Make Your Own Money

Make
YOUR OWN
Money

Shine Your Light with
Purpose and Balance

CHARLOTTE FRIBORG

NEW YORK

LONDON • NASHVILLE • MELBOURNE • VANCOUVER

Make Your Own Money

Shine Your Light with Purpose and Balance

© 2020 Charlotte Friborg

Published in New York, New York, by Morgan James Publishing in partnership with Difference Press. Morgan James is a trademark of Morgan James, LLC. www.MorganJamesPublishing.com

ISBN 9781642797336 paperback
ISBN 9781642797343 eBook
ISBN 9781642797350 audio
Library of Congress Control Number: 2019947666

Cover Design Concept: Jennier Stimson

Author's Photo Courtesy: Traci Medlock

Cover and Interior Design: Chris Treccani www.3dogcreative.net

Editor: Moriah Howell

Book Coaching: The Author Incubator

Morgan James is a proud partner of Habitat for Humanity Peninsula and Greater Williamsburg. Partners in building since 2006.

Get involved today! Visit
MorganJamesPublishing.com/giving-back

Brian, Nikolai, Rebekka, and Mathias
I love and appreciate you!

Table of Contents

Foreword

The feeling of contribution; of knowing that you've given the very best of yourself toward something or someone you deeply believe in. The sensation of loving so fully and with such one-pointed focus that your individual limitations are transcended and you're temporarily transported along a powerful current of wellbeing. The feeling of laying your head on the pillow at night, knowing that you showed up in full connection with all that you are, and shined those resources toward another human being for the purpose of helping them to discover their own potential.

These are some of the exalted moments we experience along the amazing path of motherhood. The act of raising children affords us an ever-present avenue into which we can channel our love, our generosity, our creativity and our brilliance. And when we come to the stage of motherhood when our job is "to work ourselves out of a job," many of experience this as a time of loss. But it's not the loss of our children we are grieving. It's the loss of a moment-to-moment focal point that inspires us to bring forth the best of who we are.

If you are in the midst of, or on the precipice of, this essential life transition, know that you have entered an incredibly fertile and potent time of self-discovery. This is a time to allow your unique gifts, talents, interests, and time-seasoned wisdom to blossom into its fullest expression, and in a way that brings value to many more than the members of your immediate family. Is it also a time of uncertainty? Absolutely! Any time life calls us to lose sight of one shore in order to make our way to a more expansive view, great courage is required. But this is the process of expansion that is now underway.

In the same way you provided a beautiful avenue for your children's birth and nurtured them into the amazing human beings they are today, it is now time to birth a bigger expression of yourself; to expand the contribution that you make, and to witness the value of that unique contribution as it returns to you in the form of money.

Make Your Own Money Again will not only guide you through this transition, it will awaken you to long forgotten dreams and show you how to harness powerful universal laws to bring them to fruition. Rest assured that Charlotte Friborg has successfully navigated the passage from stay-at-home mom to entrepreneur, and has guided many others along this journey as well. This book will support you in realizing the depth of your inner value, and in discovering the perfect career path to manifest that value in the form of all the abundance you deserve and desire.

Christy Whitman
New York Times *Best Selling Author and Founder,*
Quantum Success Coaching Academy
ChristyWhitman.com

Introduction

Hi! I am so happy you are here. Before you even start reading, I want to congratulate you for trusting yourself and picking this book. You will not be disappointed you did! Being a woman and mom and wanting to juggle life and make money can be a big deal. Making the transition can be even bigger. It is so easy to forget to make time for ourselves or feel we are not enough. We may even feel guilty for the things we do not do.

But that is over soon! Just stay with me. It is about making money, but it is also about so much more – OK, this will totally make sense as you read along.

Since I decided to create this book, my focus has been giving as much value as possible to everything I have learned, practiced, taught, and coached for a total of twenty-plus years. I may give you some surprises you did not expect, just like it was a surprise to me every time I learned something new. There may also be content that you have heard about before and maybe even know how to implement in your life. What I will ask you to do is be open and put everything together in the way that works best for you!

I have my life.

You have your life.

This book is intended to be adaptable to your life.

I once thought that in order to have success of any kind, you either had to be lucky or born to the right parents or with some special skills that not everyone was born with.

I know now (and soon you will too!) that success of any kind does not have anything to do with that. Your definition of success does not depend on your past or your current situation. I dare say already, before you have started the first chapter, that you can have it all. You can be the best mom, earn money, be a great spouse, have lovely friends, take care of your home, go on adventures, take care of your body, and whatever else is on your list of things that are important to you. The way to have it all may not be the way you thought. Let's begin the journey in Chapter 1 by getting to know each other.

Just promise me one thing: stay until the end, as the book is like a circle. You want it to be complete.

Enjoy!

Chapter One

So Happy We Meet

You know the expression "when the student is ready, the teacher shows up"? I have had many conversations with women who, for various reasons, would like to make their own money. It could be to just do something and feel that they contribute. It could be that they want to be able to travel more. For you, it may be because you have that desire to do something that you and your husband don't necessarily always agree on. You may have that seed of a dream inside to create something that seems out of sight because of all the other chores you have.

I know you struggle with wanting to have more. You know you have a great life and can't really complain. You had your dream fulfilled to be able to stay home for some years with your kids, and your husband supported that while he made the money. Maybe you already make some money but are not happy with what you make or your situation in general.

As time goes on, we all change. No two days are the same. New ideas and dreams are constantly planted within us. You start to feel restricted. There are things you really would like to do or have that you do not like to ask your husband for. The desire to make your own money grows and so does the reminder of that you, who years ago believed it would be possible to get back and have a career. Even one you really feel will fit your life. I want to say that it is important you listen to your inner voice and trust it. No matter what other people say, believe your inner voice.

Way too often people, especially women, sacrifice their inner voice. We do and become everything for others first. What if we could both do the amazing things for ourselves and still do great things for others?

It is all about shifting our beliefs.

Before I learned what I am going to share in this book, I felt scared and intimidated about my big dreams. I know quite a lot of women who doubt they can have what they want. They have some very special gifts, interests, and personal talents but over the years have stuffed the dream away. I think that is so sad, and I intend to support as many women as possible (including you!) to be brave and vulnerable.

I believe we all have a purpose in life. I believe we all can find something to do that gives us meaning. I've had conversations with women who almost forgot their true dreams, and they leave our conversation saying that they have started seeing possibilities again. That makes my heart sing.

What about you? Are you ready to awaken your dream and start (at your own pace) to make money and create a life that feels meaningful at a deep level? It is not about the amount of money. It's about feeling you have the freedom to buy or do what you want without having to ask your husband what he thinks.

I remember the first 2,000 dollars that rolled into my bank account after I had not made money for years. It felt amazing, even though I did not have to work because my husband earned well.

Do you have those thoughts about what your friends will say or think if you take a job to make your own money? You are not alone. That is so normal! But what do you live this life for? To stay in your seat and avoid making other people uncomfortable for fear of what they think? Or to step into doing what you truly love and feel you live your life fully? It may not be perfect. But just the fact you take action may make you feel more alive and give some meaning instead of continuing to wait.

This book may very likely change your life. I know that is a huge statement. But I dare to say that only a very small percentage of the world's population know about what's in this book. One of the biggest reasons why many hold back is the fear of success. Can I handle it? What will other people say? I personally did go through some fear of sharing part of the content I have put in this book, but now I know the power of knowing it. Not just for myself, but also for my family, the people I have coached, and those I have touched with the messages. I must share it. A big part of what I will share with you in this book, I have learned after many years of struggle. I have adopted the tools and principles one by one into my everyday life and seen how they have changed the way I perceive life, the world, and people. Let's just put it this way: it's honestly a huge part of why I feel at peace in almost in any situation. Better than that, I know that we all can create the life we truly dream about. We can have it all. I know I can trust that what I want will come.

I will teach you this. It's not a get-rich-quick scheme. It is a lifestyle where you will feel like the driver in a smoother ride through life; it becomes easier to take the twists and turns when they show up in front of you. I know how easy it is to give up your dreams when things become challenging. That contrast is a gift for more clarity. You are the one who sets the direction without feeling guilty or scared about other people's opinions and comments.

What I am asking you for now is to trust me and dare to stick it out to the end. I can't emphasize this enough. Why? Because each of these tools build upon each other. You will find the perfect job for you and make the money you want! You will let it grow and one day you can sit on the beach and celebrate the financial freedom you once dreamed about.

You were born into this life to enjoy it. To be happy. Not to struggle. I am not saying every moment in life will be like the smell of roses. However, you can get much clearer about what you want when you are in the midst of chaos and challenge.

I used to feel stuck in many situations. But when we learn that it is just a moment of possibility to get clarity of what we truly want in our life then, we have taken the first step to set ourselves free to get there.

You were born and given this body. I have heard many times from spiritual teachers that for every body given there were a thousand souls ready to take it. Think about that for a second and take time to imagine it is the truth. I have no proof whether this is correct or not. But just the thought of this being truth makes me feel so much more grateful for being given the opportunity to live this life. I do believe that since you are here it is not coincidence and you have a purpose.

Do you sometimes feel that urge to do things? Ideas popping up where you may take a few seconds to follow the thought and, if you really notice and feel it, you know that it would be amazing if you could do it. Well, let me tell you something, you can! There are more than seven billion people on this planet. You are the only one like you. There is not one single other person who is like you. Why should you not be able to have what you want?

Again, this is not a get-rich, quick fix book. It is a book to learn some basic universal principles and tools that when put together will transform your life and make it easier. I have manifested a job by just becoming crystal clear on what I wanted and when. After doing that, I received a phone call and landed the job. It was the easiest thing. That never happened in my life before. Some may say it is luck. I know it wasn't. I will teach you how. In situations where things have been tough in our family, and we needed help with something, I have used the same principles to call in the person we needed at that time.

So, if you want a job, if you want to start a small business, if you want to make money one way or another, you can do it and you can do it without sacrificing. And this is not just about accumulating material wealth, either. Because I know you, like me, do not believe in that. Of course, we can enjoy having either a lot of shoes, purses, clothes, books, or something else. But it is not about having excessively more than what we need. We also want to take care of the planet. For some years I have been focused on growing my circle of people who would like to master their life. I call it 360 Degree Life Mastery.

Making Your Wheel

Before we move on, I will introduce you to the wheel as a model of your life. I have been using this tool since 1998; I learned a lot about this from Tony Robbins.

First, you draw a circle. This symbolizes the wheel on a car. From the center of the circle and out to the outer edge it is divided into sections. Each section represents an area of our life. So, for example, I divide my life into eight areas:

- Intimate relationship
- Family
- Self-care (body, mind, spirit)
- Money
- Career
- Social life
- Society
- Home

For some years, my career was put on hold because I chose to be home with my kids. I literally imagined taking that piece out of the wheel like a piece of a pie and putting it up on a shelf for years until I was ready to pull it back out again. Those years, the part of my life where I contributed with volunteer work in our society, took a bigger chunk of my time than now when I am working again. At the time when I chose to not work, I was happy about it because since my husband and I share bank accounts we had equal access to "our" income.

If there is a life area that you really want to improve and you do not do anything about it, you will suffer. Whether you work or not, money is still a part of your life. We cannot deny money. It is part of our world. The moment you claim that you want to make your own money again, something in the universe will shift and receive your asking. You take the now missing piece of the wheel and fill it in. Your job is to ask for what you want, and then things around you will shift, and when you take action you get more clarity. You've got this book in your hand. How did you find it? Because the answer to the part of you who is ready to learn, and find that ideal job, career or new business idea to grow is here.

I just invite you to look at the circle of your life as a whole. 360 degrees. All this is you. And you will want to nurture each area and you can do that. Not everything in one go, but in this book you will receive the insights on how to fill your life areas with a job and money and kids.

Chapter Two

All is Good

How do we end up doing what we do? If we change direction, will that slow us down? When I talk to women about their careers, they have often come to a stage in their life where they realize that the choice they made about their education five years or so ago no longer fits into the life they live. But after we have kids, many priorities and responsibilities change. We are now in a situation we could not predict when we chose our path years earlier. For some, that can be intimidating and almost paralyzing. Not that the situation is intimidating itself, but because we do not know consciously how to handle when things change. It is easy to be affected by other people's expectations of us. In reality, we live in a world that is changing faster than ever, and almost nothing is predictable other than that rapid change is inevitable. Therefore, inner wisdom is so important and it comes from the connection to our inner voice, our soul, and our intuition.

I was at my first real, deep personal growth seminar in 1998, learning about how to find "the key to the future." I was hooked on learning as much as possible about self-development, time management, spirituality, and mindset, and later I started studying skills to master money. That seminar was a pivotal moment for me; I realized how powerful we are. It opened up the way I looked at how we can create our future. I will share a bit of my professional and personal journey with you so you have an idea of where my desire to coach women to step into their power and shine their light comes from.

My parents had a furniture store, and even though I had received acceptance to college to study pharmaceutical science, I chose, to my high school advisor's big dissapointment, to accept an apprenticeship with schooling in a high-end designer and furniture store. I enjoyed serving customers who invested a significant amount of money into their interior design. I also learned all aspects of running a business. After almost three years, I realized that the hours and future in retail were problematic for the life I wanted to create. I quit my job and moved to another part of Denmark where I earned what I believe is the American equivalent to a bachelor's degree in sales and marketing. I met my husband, Brian, there. This was twenty-six years ago.

We moved to England for a couple of years where I worked as a project leader in the marketing department of DuPont, an American organization. I was offered a leadership role in our department to integrate team building as a culture. This awakened my conscious awareness, curiosity, and understanding of people: Why we are different and what makes people connect and work together? I cultivated my deep desire to work with people during this time.

Back in Denmark, I soon became pregnant with our first child, Mathias. I was certain I wanted to continue working with people and took different short-term roles in bureaus assisting companies hiring people. When our son was one year old, I started a two-year study to earn my NLP master practitioner in therapy and communication.

This helped me understand at a deep level the importance of taking full responsibility for our lives and taking ownership of our own destinies. Until this time in my life I had felt like a victim of my childhood and upbringing, and was not aware of how unique each and every single one of us are and how much potential we have within us. Learning the lessons from our past, forgiving, and letting go can really work miracles in how we open up for new things in our lives.

One of my fellow NLP co-students was Sofia Manning, who invited me to participate as a student at her first coaching certification program in Denmark. At that time, she did this with another fellow student, Lonnie Borgstroem. That was my introduction to coaching.

For a few years, I had my own small company in Denmark where I was coaching and doing consulting work in how to build a strong culture between staff and leadership in a company. I did this until I gave birth to our daughter, Rebekka. Then I decided to close the company and stay home. We had our third child, Nikolai, nineteen months later.

After seven years in Denmark, Brian and I decided to say yes to a new adventure and moved our family to Florida. This is now twelve years ago.

This move gave me the opportunity to continue to stay at home with the kids, which was a dream come true for me.

Since we had our first born and I decided to not focus as much on my career, I knew it would never be too late to create a career again, even if it would be in my mid-forties. I also believed I wanted and could start a career that would make an impact on other people's lives.

It helped me a lot that we moved to an area where many other moms stayed home with their kids. This is not common in Denmark where a mom and dad are given a year's paid maternity leave. There I did not know any women who stayed home for years without being paid through social welfare or having their own business. It has been more ingrained in Danish women to stick to their career even after having children. Even though I had never been drawn to the American culture before I came here, I had this idea that it was all about big cars, houses, burgers, and Coca-Cola. I found out early that it was the ideal place for me to be a stay-at-home mother, and I learned early on about the power of gratitude, which I will come back to later.

All these years gave me an opportunity to give 1,000+ hours of volunteer work, mainly in my kids' schools.

Through being involved, I got to know a lot of people and build friendships. We had a dog, my first ever, and I went to training classes with her for years and went through a top test to get her certified so I could work with her as a therapy dog team. I started Taekwondo with my three kids and went all the way to earn the first degree black belt.

I am so grateful for my husband's support in my staying home for all those years. For him trusting me to take care of, I dare to say, everything that had to do with the kids, home, and money.

But after some years, I started feeling the urge to make my own money. As much as my husband and I easily agree on many purchases and decisions on money, we also have some different beliefs. Not making money started to make me feel limited. The desire to start a career again was born. Not just for the money, but also to start a career with something that was meaningful to me and would still fit my lifestyle and priority to be able to be here for the kids. I knew I wanted to get back to some kind of coaching, because it was still so ingrained in me to see possibilities and other people's potential.

I want to let you know that as easy I first thought it would be to start my career and business in the US, I later realized it was not easy to transition into a new country and also have a new career. I did not really realize this until I had said yes and was in the middle of it all.

We all have beliefs about what is possible and what is not, and what is easy and what is not. Until we start work consciously with our minds and get to know what is really going on inside of them, it can be quite challenging to control them.

Sometimes when we do not make things happen in our life by hesitating, or we do not know how to make them happen, we may not be aware that old limiting beliefs can be the hidden skeleton inside us. We will procrastinate or not even consider doing what we get inspiration to do.

As shared earlier, I consciously chose to be a stay-at-home mom for years. The transition back to work, however, was not easy. I have spoken to moms who've shared how difficult it was for them being a stay-at-home mom after working for years. Transitioning out of what our brain is used to can be challenging because a part of our brain wants us to stay where we are to protect us. But I believe that by focusing on what we want and how we want to feel we can create massive shifts in our life. It is our job to practice sticking to the vision and not be distracted and give up.

I am very aware that one of the main reasons it was so important for me to be with our children when they were little had to do with my own upbringing. My mother became pregnant with me when she was eighteen, and for the first few years of my life I stayed with my grandparents because my mom moved to another town to pursue her education.

As small children, we form the foundation of our beliefs about ourselves and the world we live in. Up to seven years old, our brains are developing all the beliefs and skills at various levels that will be a foundation for our life from there.

From these early childhood experiences, I had developed some pretty strong and deeply rooted beliefs about my existence. That for a mom choosing to work and focus on a career meant that she could not be there for her child. I had not felt loved. Do you see the correlation?

For many years I felt like a victim. I was upset with and angry at my mother for not showing up as I had wanted. It was painful for many years.

Today I know she did her very best. Today I am actually super proud of her and deeply grateful she chose to be strong and trusted my grandparents to take care of me.

I believe we all have some kind of story that shapes us and affects how we think and act in both ways that support us in achieving our goals but also often unconsciously sabotage us. The great thing is that we do not have to be stuck in our past. We can turn any past situation into a learning experience and become more resourceful in our future journey

The pivotal moment in my life was when I learned to take complete responsibility for my life and stop being a victim of my childhood. In the beginning, it was difficult for me to absorb that we truly are 100 percent responsible for our lives right now. I had played the same record for so many years of being a victim and accusing others when things were difficult in my life. But when I finally got it, it was the moment in my life when I set myself free. Because then we can also decide where we want to go. We have the power of our thoughts and what we speak and do. We become the driver in the car.

You might not yet be ready to totally grasp that you truly are responsible for your life, and are the master of it whether you like it as it is now or not. But now is the time. In the next chapter, I will share with you the steps to making this possible and help you to open up your mind to grasp how lucky you are to be you! How lucky you are having been through, and maybe still going through, struggles. You can relax and trust that it is all fine and how it is supposed to be and it cannot stop you in creating the life you really dream about.

Just one warning: this doesn't mean that life will be perfect moving forward. It never will. Thinking we can have perfection is an illusion and also a way of sabotaging us in getting the results we want. I will give you the tools to not be stuck and feel victimized. You can now step into your power of that phenomenal woman you were born to be. You do not have to feel guilty for wanting more. You were born to have it all.

Chapter Three

Solution Frame

Have you ever wondered why sometimes things seem easier than other times? Why is it that some days seem to flow easier? Or what about those magical moments when you think about someone and that same person gives you a call? Why does it seem like life is so much easier for others than you?

When I started to learn about the Universal Laws or principles, I wished they would be taught to every single child in school. These Universal Laws became the glue to all the other life experiences and theories I have learned. I've chosen to share them here in Chapter 3 before Chapter 4, where I dive in will into the mindset around money.

In Chapter 5, we will get into building clarity about the direction we want and choose to go for. This is very fundamental to why you do not yet have the job and make the money you want.

After this clarity, we will go into Chapter 6 and prepare to receive what we want. This is a very important step and often overlooked. I know this may be the doorway for you to become a magnet to what you want to do, have, and be in your life. We will then continue to talk about what we can do to speed up the process of manifesting the life we dream about in Chapter 7. In Chapter 8, I will share tools to make it fun and easier to plan your life and create a healthy structure for you. In Chapter 9, I will share how we make sure to also take time to relax when we live our busy lives and now maybe have taken on another huge responsibility by having a job or business. Chapter 10 is all about building support, as well as how to protect ourselves from other people's judgment. I hear many women sharing how other people's opinions make their own decisions harder. Finally, In Chapter 11, we will learn to relax knowing that obstacles will show up but now we are equipped to not let them throw us off.

The content I have put in this book is something you can keep going back to and practicing. They are connected and overlap at the same time. You do not have to master every single step and chapter before you move on to the next. Start to take notes of what may help you the most and integrate that. Then move on to the next step and go back when you are ready to dive deeper. I find that I keep learning new details in each area.

The Universal laws and principles really support all the chapters' content, and by knowing these laws I find that we discover a knowing and trust that we do live in a very loving universe where we are supposed to have it all. The Universal Laws are the glue holding together everything in life.

When I learned these principles, my life and all the experience I had until then suddenly made sense. I am dedicating this chapter to my teacher and mentor Christy Whitman for teaching this so clearly in her Quantum Success Coaching Academy.

I'd known about the Law of Attraction from reading Rhonda Byrne's book *The Secret*. Besides the law of attraction, the Universal Laws are like when Mrs. Spider connects the lines in her web and makes it stronger. It becomes complete.

In this chapter, I will introduce you to each universal principle, or the laws of the universe. Other spiritual teachers share these laws. Deepak Chopra wrote a book called *The Seven Spiritual Laws of Success*. Should you want to go deeper and want to apply and master these universal laws, then you can reach out to me through my email address or my website that are shared at the end of this book.

I will give you information in this chapter about the seven laws. This is so you can grasp the idea that we do live in a friendly universe and that when we learn these principles we can work with the universal forces. I have left an extra law to discuss later in Chapter 10.

These laws apply into any situation and action imaginable.

Before I introduce you to these essential Universal Laws, I want to make it very clear that they do not conflict with any religion. As a matter of fact, historic religious teachers talked about many of these principles in various forms.

What you will learn from this is that you can create your life and your job, attracting the money you want and the people you want from doing the work inside of you first. It is the total opposite of how many of us were taught when growing up. Many people, including myself earlier on in life, look for evidence outside of us before we believe we can be happy or that things we want are coming to us. By really learning these Universal Laws, you will know way before you actually can see, touch, or feel anything you want to have in your life that it is on its way. How does that sound to you? Well, to me in the beginning I thought it sounded really out there. Even after I started to take note of what happened in my life and I could see how the universe really works it took me a while to find the courage to share it because I wasn't ready to handle it if people thought I was weird. As I said earlier, now I feel more pain inside of me for not sharing because I know that people need to hear this. It will make life so much more easy and fun, and who am I not to share it when I have learned it.

I invite you to get a journal and start make daily notes of observations. It is such a great way to learn this. Again, I would be thrilled to support you in going deeper with this.

Let's dive in!

Law of Attraction

It is proven through quantum physics that everything is energy and that like attracts like when we dive into studying science at a subatomic level. You are energy. The chair you are sitting in is energy. Thoughts are energy. Energy can have a different vibration. We as human beings send out a different vibration depending on the feeling state we are in. When we are depressed and fearful we send out a low vibration and when we, on the other hand, feel joy, love, and gratitude, we send out a higher frequency of vibration.

The law of attraction works like the law of gravity. We do not have to think about it. It works all the time.

When we are in a negative state of mind, we will notice more negative emotions, and our day will reflect that, like hitting more red lights when we left late because we dropped a cup of coffee on our clean pants. The lady who served us at the grocery store seemed to not care and we couldn't find what we needed so easily. It is like a boomerang. We send it out and it comes back. In life, it will come back in different forms.

Law of Deliberate Creation

Now when we know that everything is energy and that we are too, it can be confusing to know that we can choose what we want to attract. In order to do that, we must be deliberate and conscious about what we want. This is about taking ownership of our lives. Know that by taking responsibility of our own thoughts, we will change the way we feel and then we will change what energy we send out.

An example of being deliberate is to think about what we want instead of what we do not want. Something that takes a lot of time for many people to unlearn is "I am tired of not making any money." This will create thought and neuro pathways in the brain to not make money. On the other hand, if you think or say "I would like to make money again," it is a total opposite statement. Try and repeat both and feel in your body the difference. The best way to start practicing this law is by asking three powerful questions throughout your day. One: What do I want? Two: Why do I want it? Three: How do I want to feel? By taking time to feel the essence of having what you want and why you want it, you will start to shift your vibration and, therefore, attract new ideas, people, and situations that will bring you closer to your goal or that of which you desire.

Law of Allowing

If we want to become masters of letting the universal laws work with us, this law is very essential and can be the hardest one for many to learn. This is about opening up to allow things to come into our life, as well as to allow for other people to be who they are. It's about accepting yourself and others without any judgment. Allow the universe time to give us what we need at the time it shows up. This is the opposite of needing to control things on the outside. The reason why this law is so important to understand is that if we feel negative emotion, we block or slow down the energy for us to move more effortlessly towards our goals. This is how people will work harder and harder and burn out. On the other hand, when we start to work with the universe and ask deliberately for what we want and are open and allow things, ideas, and inspiration to come to us, life becomes more playful and effortless.

Law of Detachment

When we start to learn to shift our thoughts to what we want to create in our lives, many people will walk around and wait impatiently for the job or the money to show up. This is another universal law that can take some patience to master. What this law really asks for is that you detach from your expectation of how what you ask for shows up. It is your job to simply pay attention. So, for example, when I manifested my most recent part-time job, I knew what I wanted and I asked deliberately for it. Then I detached from how it would show up. You may get a phone call from a friend. You may get an idea to update your resume. You may get an inspired thought about calling a friend and sharing that you are looking for a job. Inspirational thoughts that make you feel excited are often signs from the universe. You have asked and you pick up thoughts of energy.

Law of Abundance and Sufficiency

So many people live in a mindset of lack and scarcity. With this law, you will learn to notice that you are enough and what you have in your life now is enough. You do not need more money to feel happy. You are not dependent on circumstances, people, or situations to make you feel fulfilled. Instead, start to notice on a daily basis what you can be grateful for. If you have limiting thoughts of what is possible, I invite you to start thinking about how many people are on the planet. Think about the depth and variety of nature like, for example, the stars in the sky. Think about how much money is going around. There is so much abundance. In the same way, know that you are enough. You have everything you need in order to create the life you want. When you take your time to learn these principles, you will see how your life suddenly becomes more rich at all levels. Practicing this law will help you create peace inside. Having more peace inside of where you are, and at the same time being excited about what you are in the process of becoming and having, will help you manifest more effortlessly. A book that I know has helped many people shift their mindset is Viktor Frankl's *Man's Search for Meaning*.

Start to focus on your value from the inside out. This can, for some women, take some time to really open up. But if we imagine a lotus flower inside of us, symbolizing our value, and see it opening up and feel as it opens a light start to shine and become stronger from inside of us and out, until it radiates outside of us, then the light comes from an unlimited source with pure potentiality. You have so much value, and the source from where you can receive more ideas and learn from is unlimited. I do not know how you feel. But when I take time to go within and feel the essence of this, I notice a strong shift in feeling more expanded and valuable as a person.

Law of Pure Potentiality

This relates to the previous principle. As the universe constantly expands, you are connected to the universal mind through the energy that is everywhere. It is inside of you and between us. You have the capability to grow and expand as a human being. This law will help you understand that there is no limit on what you can do, have, or be. This comes back to how you think. You may have been brainwashed to think that after forty your chances of having a great career are over. Or that it is only possible to make this amount of money in certain jobs. Or that women who have stayed home cannot make a lot of money. This belief will all affect your brain, your vibration, and what you attract. But if you let go of that limited way of thinking and instead shift your focus and train your mind, you will see that there is potential in you and others. You will soon notice a shift in your life.

A powerful way to practice tapping into the energy of pure potentiality is through meditation. When we become silent, we open up to, connect to, and receive more from the unlimited universal mind. This is a source of unlimited energy and ideas. I truly believe and have seen much evidence that when we receive an idea or inspiration from Source, or "out of the blue" as some may say, we do have what it takes to have it. Otherwise, we would not receive the idea or dream to begin with.

Law of Polarity

This law explains how the universe is built on opposites. Negative and positive energy. Day and night. Light and darkness. Up and down. In and out. Dry and wet. Black and white. Happy and sad.

In any situation, you choose your thoughts. You cannot think two thoughts at the same time, but you can choose which thought to think. Some thoughts will make you feel better; other thoughts will make you feel worse. If you are in a situation you do not like, rest assured that the opposite situation is possible. It is your job to learn how to pivot it and you do that through by thought. If you are in an unwanted situation, like, for example, in an argument around money with your partner, you can now choose where you focus your mind.

Do you choose to think "My husband makes the money and I do not," or "My husband makes the money and I will, too"?

You can choose to think "I am powerless," or "I am powerful."

We all have access to the same universal intelligence. It is our job to direct our thoughts we send out (deliberately) and we will attract a thought or idea that matches that frequency (law of attraction).

This gave you a brief introduction to the universal principles. This could take up an entire book. I will refer to these laws in the following chapters. The essence of this is for you to understand that everything is connected, and when you understand that and that you can direct your thoughts toward what you want and pay attention to your feelings, you will become the master of your own energy and life.

These laws can basically be your guidelines to learn how to create anything in your life. They can become your checklist of whether you work with the universal availability of help or against it.

Chapter Four

The Green Dust

This chapter is dedicated to money and to you if you have never been introduced to this way of thinking about money. This is a concept I am still exploring and taking in.

When you are married to someone who makes a good living and you don't have to work, it can be a challenging decision to decide to work again. I know many women who would give their left leg to stay at home.

I know that feeling of guilt for wanting more. I felt it myself until I released it and opened up for all the good things I can do with more money.

As I said, this is not a get-rich-quick book. That may be a book I write in the future. It is not even a goal of mine right now. Not that I do not want to make millions. I do. But I know I have my money stuff to work on before I get there.

We have talked about the Law of Pure Potentiality and that there can be these glass ceilings of what our brains can absorb. It is like when we exercise for a long-distance race. If we never have been running before, the belief of one day being able to run a half marathon can sound exhausting. But when we start to run and get to run ten kilometers and we hear others say that if you can run ten kilometers you can also run twenty kilometers, then it is like the glass ceiling is being lifted.

Money is energy like anything else in the world, but it does not have a meaning. Before I learned that money is just energy, I had a way different way of thinking about money. I thought the only way get it was through hard work, because I always thought that it took hard work to make a lot of money. I was tempted to look into some offers to work out of the home, but that did not really click with me. I knew that for me to start making my own money, it was important to work from home to be able to still be available as my husband travels a lot. I also wanted the freedom to take my work with me when I traveled, and at the same time I liked the freedom of being my own boss.

I chose to start my own company. Soon I learned that it required more from me than learning the skills of being an entrepreneur in today's world.

You can buy many books about how to get rich and be wealthy, and if you haven't already done so, I invite you to do it. Even people on lower incomes. like teachers, become millionaires. It is not just about making more but also giving the money a structured container to be and grow in and have consistency around.

Another thing I learned five years ago from Joe Vitale is that money likes speed. First I was like, "What?" But when I took it in and related it to the universal laws, it all made sense. I can see it in the way that if we take action and inspiration and follow through with it, more ideas start to come. Thoughts are energy. Money is energy. When we show the universe we are serious about something, it will send more.

Even though I have always had a belief that I would have enough and that I would always be supported and able to work, learning about the universal laws and money has revealed many limiting beliefs in me around it. Through stories and what we have heard and experienced around money as children, we often unconsciously carry supportive or limiting beliefs around money. When I was a kid, I remember my grandmother saying, "Don't pick that coin up, it's dirty," when I found money on the ground as we walked to my pre-school. This was an innocent comment from my grandmother in a well-meant moment. But if you think about what is really being said in that moment to a child, that could have been a moment of celebrating money showing up in her life. When I started looking into my limiting beliefs, I realized that these comments about money had affected me; I did not allow myself to receive money when it showed up. But by being conscious about these old stories about our parents, grandparents, or other influential people in our life, we can change our mindset to become more abundant around money.

Money doesn't grow on trees. Did your parents tell you that? I remember mine did. It is honestly not that as a child you don't know that, but it is a clear way of thinking there is a shortage of supply. When in reality, there is an abundance and unlimited potential. Think about this: Some forms of money are made of paper, and where does paper come from? Trees!

One of my coaching buddies shared with me that she was following this lady who taught about attracting more money. One of her exercises was to expand the brain's way of thinking and to stop limiting thoughts and instead step into the law of abundance and sufficiency by imagining all the leaves on the trees were made of money. It may sound silly, but think about it for a second. Why not? There really is an unlimited supply.

I remember I used to have a slightly dark way of thinking about rich people. I did not feel super safe or secure around them. It was like I put myself down and thought they were more and people I did not deserve to hang out with. When I looked into this, I realized I, as a child, had learned to judge people with money for being better than others. My dad would not buy a Mercedes Benz because he thought people would judge him and think he made too much money in his store. Since I have always been very sensitive, I noticed early on in life that thinking this way did not feel good.

By living with the Law of Polarity, we now also know we can just choose a thought on the other end of the spectrum. When I was a child, we did not talk about money this way and I had no other guidance or tools to lean on, other than feeling uncomfortable thinking about rich people and the idea of not having an abundance of money.

I work constantly on my money beliefs, and from studying many teachers who have made millions, it is common to continue to run into some kind of money blocks. The good thing is that when we first learn the techniques of how we can shift our mindset, it is not as hard to raise the glass ceiling.

One way of doing so is to start making the structure for money. David Bach, a famous financial author, teaches this very easy process of taking a percentage of your income and putting it into various buckets on a consistent basis. After reading it, I thought it made sense at an intellectual level, and, knowing that money is energy, it also makes sense at an energetic, emotional, and spiritual level. His biggest advice with this tool is to take a percentage of your income and give to some kind of charity. He mentions that all of the rich people he knows became rich after they started giving. This refers back to the Law of Abundance and Sufficiency.

The most important thing I have learned to open up for the floodgate of money is to appreciate it. To really take time to look at my money on a daily basis and show gratitude for whatever comes in.

I throw in this chapter to share with you that you deserve to earn as much money as you would like to. Money does not have a meaning.

It is not as if when we get a lot of money, we will become evil or mean. I totally believe, and have seen this from many I study and learn from, that what money gives us is the capability to give more.

Referring back to Law of Attraction, if you would like to receive more of something, you must send that out. So, if you would like to receive more money, give more and feel good about it. Decide today that when you make your first paycheck that you will give maybe ten percent away. That is what David Bach recommends. Many will wait and think that they will do it when they get a raise. But this is not about wanting to have more; this is about stepping into the Law of Abundance and Sufficiency and belief of Pure Potentiality. If you have never done it, I invite you to try and set up a structure where you do give ten percent to a cause every month. It can be different kinds. It feels amazing. If it doesn't make you feel better, then it will just block your energy of receiving more. In that case, take some time and look at what limiting beliefs it is time to release around money, which I will help you with in Chapter 6. Being able to give and feel good about it can be one way to allow yourself to feel rich, and by feeling rich and abundant you will attract more.

So how do we handle situations where there is something we really want but when we look at our bank account there isn't money to pay for it? Here language is important. Instead of saying "I am broke," or "I can't afford it," which tells the brain to create more of that, start say to yourself "This is not a priority," or "I choose to not buy this at this time." A powerful question to ask yourself that will help your brain to open up for new possibilities would be "How can I make the money to buy this?" This is opening up for a deliberate creation. You can now play with the idea of how it would feel. By feeling good about something you raise your vibration and open the floodgate of inspiration and ideas. On the other hand, by feeling negative emotions and restriction, we block the energy and flow of money coming to us. Later in the book we will talk about the importance of taking action.

Chapter Five

Get to Know Yourself

Anything created in the world was once a thought. A thought is energy. In today's world, most people live for validation from the outside before they take action. When we see other people's Instagram or Facebook posts, we easily compare ourselves. The inner voice, when paying attention to it, will run a long, noisy conversation: "That is better than what I have… Her husband doesn't travel so she has more time… I wish I was that lucky…" blah, blah, blah.

That is not how we create. Well, yes, that is a way of creating a life of feeling miserable and in despair, and living with envy for what other people have and regret about what we don't have. But that's not what you want to create.

I am not saying you are like that. But I know that's what happens if we forget how we were born to create. It is a way to create by default instead of with the Law of Deliberate Creation.

You were born into this world as unique as your fingerprints. You have your right and power to create your life exactly as you want it. It all starts within you. Not that there is anything wrong with Instagram or Facebook, but it is our job to pay attention to how we react to what we see. If you see someone has something you would like to have as well, know that you can have it, too. Maybe not in exactly the same form, but something that will make you feel as great as you think you would feel if you had what your neighbor or Facebook friend has.

It is time we explore our inner world and get to know and master our own energy.

As I shared with you in Chapter 2, ask the powerful questions "What do I want," "Why do I want it," and "How would I like to feel" and then feel that feeling now.

One of the processes I go back to again and again is called Clarity Through Contrast. It is from Michael J. Losier's book *Law of Attraction – The Science of Attracting More of What You Want and Less of What You Don't*. This book refers straight back to the Law of Polarity. Whenever we notice that there is something in our life we do not want it is a possibility to pivot and ask ourselves what we do want.

Let us use the conversation about making our own money in this example of how to use The Clarity Through Contrast Process. Write down all the things that you currently do not like in your life on the left side of a piece of paper. This could be:

1. Not able to buy what I want
2. Feeling powerless
3. I don't have time to work

Keep writing down everything you do not like in this part of your life. This is the contrast to what you want. On the right side of the paper, you now take each statement of contrast and ask yourself what you *do* want. Let's use the three statements above and pivot these into clarity statements:

1. I am able to buy what I want
2. I am powerful
3. I have all the time I need

When you have pivoted all the statements you wrote down on the left side you cross them out. They are gone. Now you take the clarity statements and write them into feeling statements. Like:

1. I love knowing I can buy what I want
2. It feels so expanding to feel powerful
3. I love knowing I have all the time I need

Now our brain will likely start to object with thoughts like but that is not true. And this is where your job comes in to lean into the Law of Allowing and Detachment. To soften your resistance, you can ask yourself powerful questions like, "What if it was true? How would my life be if it was like this?" It is not important to do this perfectly. What is important is that you notice and feel a shift inside of you and that you feel better.

Remember, everything created in the world was once just a thought. The job and the money you want to make are first a thought and idea before they become reality. The fastest way to find the courage to start your own business or look for a job is by putting your attention on what you want and not on your limiting thoughts where you focus on what you do not have or with envy compare yourself to others. Well, if you see someone have something you would like, instead of feeling envy now know that this is for you too and say that to yourself: "And this is for me, too." If you have never done this kind of inner work before, you may experience in the beginning that it feels awkward because it is a new way of thinking. And you may question if you're doing it right. There is no right or wrong. The best way to check in to see if you are moving in the right direction is to notice, as mentioned earlier, if you feel better.

This is like when you buy a new pair of shoes that may feel different to your old shoes. In order to break the new shoes in, you have to wear them. After continuing to wear them, they will gradually feel more natural and comfortable. In this way, your new way of thinking will become your new natural state of mastering your mind... as long you keep practicing!

My passion for more than twenty years has been to create a life with 360-degree life mastery. I imagine, since you're reading this book, that it is important for you to not just start a new career and then forget about yourself and the rest of your life. In order to master our lives we must know what that is for us. At this time in my life I feel very successful in having created a life where I have it all. Even while I am working on improving areas in my life. When I work with clients I always go back and make them define what life areas they have and draw a circle and divide the space into the amount of areas they have found, for example family, body, money, career, home, social, like the example in Chapter 1. After giving each life area a part of the circle, ask yourself how satisfied you are from one to ten. One is the center of the circle a ten is the outer edge.

For the eight years I did not work, I deliberately took career out of the circle but chose to put in my contribution to society as a volunteer, as that was a bigger part of my life during those years. Some areas may come and go, but others will always be a part of you. One is money. Even if you do not work, money is a part of your life. You cannot exist in today's world without money, whether you receive it from your husband's income or social welfare if you live in a country where that is an option.

After scoring your life, you will notice that some areas are not filled out as much as others. The next step is where the inner work comes in to write down what you really want with no limitation for each area. Be a child again. Imagine what each life area would look like if you would give it a ten.

Write down for each life area what you really want, why you want it, and how it makes you feel, and feel it now. The more you do this the more amazed you will be at how things will shift in your life. You literally program your brain to look for those answers and start noticing where to find them.

This is what creating your life from the inside means.

Your job is now to start noticing your emotions. Remember you are an energetic being and the universe will respond to how you feel. You can't ask for too much. But if you notice self-doubt kicks in, know that you will repel it because you will not be a vibrational match for it to come to you. If you have not yet found your dream job it is not because it is not possible for you to have it. It is simply because you are not clear on what it is and you focus on that, or you focus more on that you do not earn money, or maybe you have thought about what your ideal job would be but you do not trust it will happen.

For some people it can feel intimidating and challenging to let go of limiting thoughts about what is possible. Remember, it is not about creating a perfect life.

That is impossible. We will never be done. It doesn't mean we cannot stop and feel totally fulfilled in the moment now and grateful for everything we do have. As human beings, when we achieve a goal, we will naturally come up with a new desire. Therefore, we will never be done. And expecting perfection is the biggest enemy for bringing in joy in your life.

This can take time to really understand and master.

Just be patient and keep practicing. I will share a tool later in Chapter 8 that I use every single day and it really has transformed most of my life areas because it helps me to stay on track.

When you know that you create your life from the inside and when you are deliberate about what you want to create, you may realize how much hard work on the outside you will not have to do. What happens is when you tap into this way of creating your life from the inside, you actually connect with a higher power and the infinite intelligence in the universe.

In order to master this at a higher level, meditation will help you. I encourage you to start build a meditation routine. This was not easy for me but it changed my life in many areas. One of the biggest gifts I have learned from meditating is to feel and master my own energy, and also to learn to notice the energy around me. Again, like any other new tool, it takes time. I used to feel so insecure about if I was doing it correctly or not. I had a very hard time quieting my mind. You can't do anything wrong. The best start may be to find some guided meditations online. There is an abundance of free resources online. I enjoy guided meditations.

Let's go back to being a deliberate creator. When you have decided that you want to make your own money, start think about in what form you would like to make it. What is important to you when it comes to the time you work at and for how many hours? Would you like to work from home or in an office? Would you like to be employed or work more freelance with the freedom of also starting a company? Write down everything.

Something else I think is important to mention at this time is to be aware as you now step into your power of thinking in possibilities and unlimited potential. You cannot go back to how you used to live and think without feeling terrible. When you grow as a human being, you step into a new version of you. Going back and try to live like you used to will feel like torture. We are born to grow and expand, just like the universe. We cannot go back. I like the way my mentor, Christy Whitman, explains it, "It is like when you have given birth to a baby. She is there; you can't put her back in." The same counts with your ideas and dreams. Once created, they are there. Of course, you can decide to change your mind and direction. But then this will come from a deliberate and conscious stand of point and therefore feel powerful.

When making decisions, you can learn to be clearer and know what is a yes and what is a no. The most powerful way of doing so is to imagine that everything comes from light. Let's say you are in doubt about what kind of job to go for. You have some ideas but are not sure what would be the best route to take. Imagine looking at your ideas from a more energetic perspective, and ask yourself which of the ideas has the brightest light. Trust your inner wisdom in whatever comes up and follow that light. Don't stop here! Keep asking what the next thing to do will be. Wait for answers to come. You will be amazed how much infinite wisdom you have as you continue to practice this. Just know that every time you doubt your inner wisdom, your light will dim.

If you have no clue what will be the best direction to start moving forward, sit and close your eyes and go back to childhood and connect with what you enjoyed doing the most. What made you feel like you were in heaven? What made you feel alive and joyful? Explore what comes up. Ask your brain to show you memories. You will suddenly remember things you have not thought about for years. Write them down and ask yourself what this may be telling you. What could this be a sign for you to do now?

Now, when you have done this inner work, you take action. Let's say your inner child liked to speak; you may want to sign up for a speaking class or Toastmasters. Whatever ideas come up, take action on them. This is important and I will repeat this later. Sometimes the ideas we get do not make sense in our logical mind and we question them. But this is where we must trust the Law of Detachment. We do not have to know the "how" to get what we want, that is where the universe will guide us when we lean in and use the Law of Allowing to let the universe guide us. It took me time to understand. In the beginning I was very hesitant because I wanted to see proof and be able to analyze first. Or I would think about how I explained my decisions to others because I knew they would not make sense in the world most people live in. Trust me on this. Make a note and we will get back to more steps so at the end of the book you will feel complete with having the answers to the questions that may pop into your head now.

Chapter Six

Create a Void

If you want to fill a pond with fresh, clean water, you must first have or create a structure and have it empty it to fill it up.

If we want to receive more, we must be willing to let go of more. It is how the entire universe functions. Like your breath. In order to breathe in fresh air, you make room inside by breathing out.

Thirty years ago, when I found the very first article about decluttering and how it affects our wellbeing, I was still living in Denmark. I did not know all the things I know now. Feng Shui and the whole awareness about decluttering was not as known as it is today in the Western world. But for some reason, I was attracted to this article and started noticing how I felt when I cleaned out my cabinets, drawers, and closet. At that time I was quite amazed and wondered what it was about.

I am sure you have experienced the uplifting feeling of finally getting your office desk cleaned after papers have been piling up for weeks. But cleaning out is not just done physically in our homes. It is also an internal job. For example, something that regularly needs to be cleaned up are those limiting beliefs we have been talking about. These are the thoughts we have at a conscious or unconscious level about what we believe is possible or not.

I remember when I considered opening up for my career life area. I thought my kids would be disappointed. It was what I believed. I thought they would feel I neglected them. But in reality, the day I told them I wanted to become a coach again and take a new certification to upgrade my skills and language, they were thrilled. When I later decided to find a part-time job on the side, they were thrilled, too. They were happy for me. And I am sure they were happy because they could feel it was in alignment with where I was in my life.

Do you have areas where you hold back because you do not want to disappoint others? I have spoken to other women for whom the transition to going back to work is difficult.

So letting go of my belief that I would not be as supportive as a mother to my kids opened up for more joy and satisfaction. Can you see how this works?

I've also spoken to women who have had a career from when their kids were born and spent much time feeling guilty for working and having less time with them. When they later had a conversation with their now-adult kids about how they felt, many shared that their kids were grateful that they had been working and it had helped them to develop more independent life skills.

We often spend so much time questioning and doubting ourselves. If we spend the same amount of time and energy tapping into what we want in our life and taking action toward creating that, we would avoid so much frustration and regret and so many self-destructive thoughts.

Forgiving your past is another way to create space within you.

What happens when we let go of past negative experiences is that we create a vacuum. We can compare it to when we have forgotten to change the bag in the vacuum and how slowly it sucks up the dirt that way, but the moment you put a new empty bag in, the vacuum sucks up way better.

This is how it works:

If you want more money, give more money.

If you want more clothes, let go of things in your closet you do not use.

I recently set up new bank accounts to start a retirement savings and regular savings from my business income. Just the shift of taking action on setting up this structure immediately attracted new business possibilities.

We can also clutter our time and calendar in a way that we do not allow in appointments that will benefit us. If you want more time for what is important, let go of what is not so important.

Forgive your past. Holding onto old hurts and blame is just creating internal clutter. Let go and stop pointing fingers and blaming your mother, husband, kids, or other people for not having what you want. Maybe they have said something that hurt you. Maybe someone did something that was really painful. Forgiving and moving on doesn't mean you accept the behavior. But it sets you free to focus on what you want instead. There are various processes to work with forgiveness. The way to work with forgiveness depends on you and how deep it is. Therapy or some modality of healing work can be a way to work with the deeper forgiveness work. Emotional Freedom Techniques (EFT) and Ho'oponopono are powerful tools that can be done easily and without negative consequences. There is a lot of information about them online if you do not know how they're done. I have personally healed a lot of childhood trauma by using these techniques. Also by going deep in guided meditations, as well as by using hypnosis.

Therefore my dear friend, own your dream and create space for it. Be conscious about what you hold onto in life and start noticing if it supports you in achieving your dream or if it's time to let go. We will talk more about what we then choose to do instead when we have created this vacuum in the next chapter.

There are so many books about how to declutter. There is no right or wrong way. If you feel like a mess inside right now, don't panic or think you can't make positive change. Start with one little area. I tell you that just the small shifts will make a huge difference. Again, what is important is to notice if you feel better by doing so. By starting to take action, you are telling the universe you are ready for more. Making it a habit to do small things on a daily or regular basis is better than being overwhelmed and thinking you have to do it all at once. Feeling overwhelmed will just block your energy of receiving what you want. I use the mantra "perfectly imperfect action." This is such a powerful reminder to get started instead of expecting perfection and being overwhelmed and not getting started. I would love to hear what your experience will be from just doing this part of what I am sharing in the entire book.

Chapter Seven

Upgrade and Prepare

N ow, when we have become clear on what we want and have created a void or vacuum to be more attractive and magnetic to the new future we would like to magnetize into our lives, the next powerful step is to start be the person who already has this dream future.

As I mentioned in Chapter 3, I truly believe that when we get a desire or have a dream we have what it takes to get it. In order for you to prepare to receive what you will attract I will share some of my favorite strategies.

Make a document that you can call "My Uniqunesses," "I am a hero," or something else that resonates with you. The idea is to create a document with a list of all of your accomplishments and unique personality traits. It can contain everything you've learned and experienced, and I want to underscore everything. All of your certifications and roles. If you have notes from family, friends, clients, or co-workers, gather them all together in a document. I do not want you to hold back. Imagine it was your best friend putting this together for you to celebrate you and your life. Do this for yourself. Notice how that feels. If any resistance come up, do what it takes to let go of that. Keep this document and take it out on the days where you feel doubtful and question what you are capable of.

When we want to work deliberately with the universe and attract what we want in our life, it is important to understand that we are the masters of our own energy. In Esther and Jerry Hicks' *Ask and It Is Given*, they teach about how we, with various processes, can move our emotions up the vibrational scale. There is nothing wrong in feeling sad or angry. What matters is if you stay in the energy and start to feel worse because you do not know how to change your emotions. When you start to be a deliberate creator and pay more attention to your emotions you will know that you do not ever have to feel stuck again. There is nothing like stuck other than having it as a belief.

I am mentioning it here because when we prepare for receiving what we want it is important to notice how we feel. Do we feel positive and trust the job and the money will show up? Or are we anxious and doubtful we will manage to find the job we really would like? It is your job to learn to master your energy. When you feel positive about a new goal and intention you have set and are in alignment with it, the chance you will manifest it faster is higher. As a matter of fact, Abraham says that if we had no resistance in the form of doubt or negative emotions, then things would manifest instantly. That is how fast the universe can work.

I definitely recommend this book. It was a huge eye-opener for me when I entered the magical world of learning to work with the universal laws and energy.

Another way to keep your vibration high is to make it a priority to do things you like. Things that make you feel great, whether it is taking a walk in nature, listening to music and dancing, reading books, painting, meditating, or exercising.

You can also start to upgrade your environment. Throw out your old towels and buy some new ones. Use the underwear, jewelry, and clothes you keep for a special occasion.

Meditation is my biggest recommendation. It really is such a great tool to connect with yourself, release, call in energy, and reset yourself. I have healed pain in my body from meditating.

A guided meditation in particular I like after having set new intentions and goals is to connect with your future self. We all have thousands or unlimited versions of our future self. She can show up in all versions depending on what decisions and actions she takes now and after. Take a few minutes to close your eyes and do what you need to relax. Imagine you are at a very peaceful place in nature where it is only you and you know no one else will show up. Imagine thousands of lights on the horizon. One is bigger than the others. This is your ideal future self when you have found the ideal way of making your money, through a job or career or business you really enjoy, have the money in the bank, and still manage to live a fulfilled life where you exercise, spend time with your family and friends, travel, and enjoy your life. See her come closer and closer until she is right in front of you. Now notice how she looks. How she is dressed. How confident she looks and sense her energy. This is you. Now step into her body. Just take the time you need. Feel how that feels. Notice how your future self is thinking, what her beliefs are, how she feels. Feel her high vibration. Allow yourself to really be her for a moment. Then, when you step out of her again and stand in front of her, imagine a line of light between her third eye in the middle of her head between her eyebrows and your third eye. Between her heart and your heart and between her power center and your power center. Notice that you are connected. If she was going to say something, give you advice or a gift, what would that be? Remember, this is very real. Time in the past, now, and the future is simultaneous. You have already created what you want.

How was that?

Remember, we talked in the beginning of the book about how all things first were a thought. It is your job to raise your glass ceiling and allow in all the good to come. You can have, be, and do whatever you want, but only if you are ready to receive it. The universe is always friendly and only wants the best for you.

Chapter Eight

Money Likes Structure

So when we prepare to receive our desires and make the foundation, there are different things I find very supportive to keep me moving forward and not let it be another pipe dream. In this chapter, we will work on how we keep the structure and build successful habits to build momentum in our lives. We do not want to continue having these amazing ideas and then just find ourselves once more sitting on the couch, realizing that it did not become our reality once again.

In all the years I have been studying ways to get the most out of time, there are some models from some teachers that stand out and have helped me to be more effective and feel I more or less get to manage my entire life in a way I am super proud of today. It is not perfect, but I know I take massive perfectly imperfect action and get results from it.

Have you ever read Steven Covey's books? He teaches a time management grid that helped me to be conscious about how I spend my time. You look at four different ways you spend your time.

1. Important and not urgent. This is where you want to spend majority of your time. These are things you plan. When you plan and are a deliberate creator of your life, you will over time live more and more of your time in this area.
2. Urgent and Important. This is when a pipe in the house suddenly breaks. These are things we must take care of. We can over time minimize these things to happen by deliberately taking time for maintenance.
3. Urgent and not important. These are things we often think are important but really are not. Many

people who are not productive spend a lot of time here thinking what they do is very important, but it really is not.

4. Not urgent and not important. This is the time we spend on social media and where we just do something to remove ourselves, such as watching TV. We think we need it. But it is often just a distraction and avoidance instead of prioritizing what is really important for us and will make a difference in our lives.

When we start to question what we spend our time doing, we can start to be more conscious and find lot of extra hours throughout our week to work on making our dreams a reality.

Tony Robbins also included this grid when he taught his time management system that he calls OPA. In this teaching, he says to not just focus on the activities but also on the outcomes of what we want.

Today I have learned to ask some powerful questions when I move around my day. A question like, "Does this make me move closer to or further away from my goal?"

There are lots of ways to be more time efficient and get more out of a day.

I have studied and tried a lot of systems and from them found my own system that works well for me now.

I think the biggest gift we can give ourselves is to take time at the end of the day to evaluate the day. I divide it into sections.

1. What worked well
2. What didn't work out so well
3. How can I get this done or what can I do to solve it
4. When will I do something about it, and then I schedule that

By taking time each day to do this, I find that I spend very little time on firehosing.

Spending time to celebrate successes from each day is essential, too. This is a way to live and celebrate the law of abundance. A success can be a nice event or moment, a goal you achieved, a new client, or someone contacting you with a new contact person. You can celebrate that you got your exercise done. Nothing is too small or too big to be celebrated. I always write down at least three things every day that I am grateful for, a win, a success, or a miracle where something suddenly happened that is obviously that the universe answering my question. The power comes when we take time to feel the gratitude of the things we have written down.

During the time at night I call my hour of office power, I always take a look at my finances. I track the money that went out and came in. I feel gratitude for my money, even when I owe money. Then I feel gratitude for the trust the bank gives me.

A system that works very well for me is to have a notebook where I write down everything. I buy the notebook in a size that easily fits into almost any of my purses. This is the book I use to plan my day. Every night, I create a page for the next day with my life areas listed and then I figure out what I will do in each life area. At the bottom of this page is where I each night write down my success, wins, and gratitude notes. During the day when I get ideas or take notes I use this book. This way I do not have 1,000 sticky notes all over my office and home. I got inspired to carry a notebook with me by Richard Branson, founder of the Virgin Group, when I read one of his books years ago.

Besides the notebook, I also print a sheet with my success habits in a chart each month. These habits have been growing over the years. The chart is made as a grid where there is a square per day for the entire month. Each night I check of which of my success habits I have done. By having this sheet, I do not forget what habits I know will support me. Often when we hear a good idea that we want to do for ourselves, like to start eat five greens every day, we forget about it after a few days. But by having it written down, we see it every day. There is much power for the brain in these visual tools. I have used this success habit sheet for almost four years now. I have shared it with many who tell me how it helps them stay on track.

Another powerful tool I can recommend that I use a lot is to pre-pave your day. Now we know we live in a friendly, abundant universe with pure potentiality, and see that where we put our attention things will grow.

This is done best in segments, which means smaller chunks of the day. The way to do it is to visualize how you would like a particular part of your day to unfold. Imagine it as real as you can where you also step into the situation and feel it happening. This process or exercise will save you much outer work. Did you know that one hour of inner work equals seven hours of outer work?

I know you like to have various projects going and things can sometimes be overwhelming. Then it is time to ask for help from your manager. Guess who that is? The universe! If you have a long list of things to do – stop.

Take a fresh page in your notebook, if you use one like me, or a piece of paper works great, too. Write down all the things you need to do. Now, take each item and ask if this is something you have to do yourself today, or tomorrow if it is the night before. If you are the only one who can do this task, write it down as a task you will do. If this can be done by someone else, make another list that you call your Universal Manager. Put as much over to the Universal Manager as possible. Now it is your time to remember Law of Detachment and let go and trust the Law of Allowing that this thing will be taken care of. I can't remember how many times it has happened to me that the people I need to talk to calls me or I meet them or someone else does it. Try it.

Again, when creating structure in your life, remember that you live in a Universe of Polarity and contrast will always show up. Things happen that we must deal with at the most unexpected or unwanted times. But know that there is a divine timing we are not in control of. If you can start to practice not being the victim but trust that the situation did not occur unless you could handle it – stop. Breathe, release, and meditate. And use this opportunity to ask for what you want, instead of being a victim and feeling sorry for yourself.

Chapter Nine

Action is Needed

I used to run around from when I woke up until I went to bed like I was stuck in a hamster wheel, doing all the things I thought were very important and urgent. In my brain, I was always on my way to the next thing. This was partly a habit deeply ingrained in me from hearing my mom's belief that you must work before pleasure.

Today I believe almost the opposite. As I mentioned in the previous chapter, one hour of inner work equals seven hours of outer work.

We need both, and it is like the Law of Polarity. We will never see any results if we just sit and journal, meditate, create vision boards, and dream all day long. We must also follow through on the ideas we receive and do some physical work.

After many years of constantly doing, doing, doing, one day I ended up driving to the ER because I seriously thought I was sick. I had pain in my chest and tingling through my left arm. I was burned out. Not to an extent where I could not function, but my body said, "Stop!"

Not long after, I started meditating and experienced the calmness and peace it gave me. I noticed how my creativity and intuition became stronger. Learn to balance doing and being. You will eventually get to know yourself enough so that you know when you are out of alignment and need to re-center yourself with mediation or other inner work exercises.

The formula for manifesting is to do both. I promise you that if you start following your intuition and follow through on the ideas that you receive from your connection with the universal mind, you will get more and more. Because you as a physical being are the vessel for the universe to live the purpose your soul wants you to do. Another example of the Law of Polarity: your physical being and nonphysical being. Isn't it just interesting and beautiful.

Have you ever heard about Dr. Masaru Emoto's *Water Experiment – Words are Alive*?

It is an experiment with water being frozen when exposed to positive words or negative words. The water will form beautiful ice flower crystals when exposed to positive words. When exposed to negative words, the water would not form a pattern but just freeze with a more ruptured form. In the same way, he played music of different genres and the water would freeze into different shapes. This experiment is proof of the power of our words.

The importance of taking action is worth repeating at this point. When we learn the importance of doing the inner work, it can become such a freeing new awakening and it is easy to fall into the trap of forgetting the action part because it feels so good and amazing to meditate or journal. I know I fell into this trap after my years in the hamster wheel. I could suddenly breathe again. I stayed there for a long time. Until I realized I had forgotten to also do things. Take action. It may sound like a joke, but I am not kidding. It is normal. You have a left side and a right side. A feminine side and a masculine side. The feminine is the being part and the masculine the doing part. Use both to stay in balance.

Imagine if you tried to only walk with one leg in front all the time. It is impossible. You wouldn't get anywhere. You walk by using left, right, left, right, and so on.

Sometimes then when we start opening up and working with the universe, we get all these ideas and have to choose what is most important, and it becomes critical to make smart choices. Make decisions and trust those decisions. Something I learned from my teacher and mentor, Christy, is to look at the choices like roads or lines of lights in front of me. When I look at the different choices, which of the paths has the most light? That's the one to choose. I know it can sound weird, but when you open up to seeing these things you really start to see the light. I know you can. Just be patient. I honestly believe you read this for a reason. Just start pay attention to all the signs you receive. The universe literally is guiding you. But it is your job to make the decisions. We are co-creators with the universe. Again, you are a physical being with an energetic connection to all that is. Isn't that just powerful?

So remember, you do not have to do it all. Your job is to be clear as to what you want. Ask and detach from how it will manifest or happen and when. The how is not your job. That is where you get assistance from the universal manager. Please have fun with this.

Chapter Ten

Your Support

When I started learning all these new amazing tools and principles, I was so ready to go out into the world, and wanted everyone to know about it. But not everyone is ready to hear about this. At the same time, I also experienced a fear of what the people who clearly had not been introduced to working with the universal laws would say or think about me and I held back.

Today I have no fear of sharing what I know because I have practiced it for so long that I know it works. I no longer care if people do not like me for what I stand for. As long as I feel integrity inside of me, it is ok. Does that mean my life is perfect? Heck no! I am still working on raising my glass ceiling and stepping into new future versions of me. I think that is something we can do for the rest of our lives.

What I will encourage you to do is to find people who will support you in following through on your new standards for yourself.

I like to compare a new idea or goal we have to a seed we plant in the ground. A small, fragile seed. Would we plant this seed in the middle of the field where the farmers market takes place each Sunday and people would be stepping across the spot where seed will soon start to grow? No way! We would put a fence around it to protect it and keep an eye on it to make sure it gets enough water and nutrients.

Can you see how this can be your metaphor for remembering to be super gentle and kind to yourself when you set new goals and intentions?

Your fence can be many of the tools in this book. But you should still find people who will support you. And even better, find people who already have what you are going after, like coaches, trainers, and mentors. I cannot say this enough. The times in my life where I had the biggest results were the times when I invested in help from people who were there to support, push, cheer me on, set the structure, or do whatever I needed.

Have you ever bought a gym membership? I have several times in my life. Going to the gym is not my cup of tea. The only time when I had success with a fitness membership was when I also hired a personal trainer. I had found a physical trainer who put together a schedule that had variety and it just made it more fun. Of course I could have gone to the gym on my own and done the same things But I did not. When I was with her she held me accountable. Plus, there is something magic that happens when you pay for something. Money is an energetic exchange of value. If what you pay matches the value you get and you take this seriously, I bet the chance of better results is ninety-nine percent.

Have you heard the old phrase that you will become the average person of the five people you hang out with the most? Think about that. Who do you hang out with? This doesn't mean you should trash all your old friendships. No, definitely not. Old friendships can also help you stay grounded, as long they support your new you. But if there is an area you want to grow find your support system.

And remember you do have your Universal Manager.

Support in achieving your daily task or bigger long term goals also depends on your daily habits. Make sure you take breaks and do things you enjoy. Having fun and joy is what life is about. That can be your emotional and energetic support system you create for yourself.

Maybe by reading this far, you can see that there is really not just one way to create an amazing and fun life while you make money and shine your light. But there are many ways. It is up to you to test, try, keep learning, and see what works for you and what doesn't. I could fill in so many more exercises, but have chosen to share in this book what I sense this is what you may like the most at this time. But I would love to hear from you about what you found out works for you to be the powerful woman who has it all.

Chapter Eleven

Obstacles

When we decide to step into a new role in our life, it is natural to feel excited for a short while and take action but then fall back into old habits.

Part of our brain likes to keep us where it knows us best. I call it the lizard brain. It is the primitive amygdala that has helped us to survive at times when we lived more predictable lives with not so many opportunities and change as we experience in the world today. When life was more about just surviving than thriving as we experience today when we have all our basic needs met. This brain has not developed and is still trying to protect us.

But we can still grow and step into a bigger version of ourselves by taking action. Many people think they need confidence before they can start. But you build confidence by taking action. Again, this goes back to receiving inspiration for things you can do to find the perfect job or make more money. By taking action, you learn new things and meet new people. Sometimes things don't turn out as you thought they would. Then you just use this awareness to adjust and take a new path. But people may comment on you and not like that you change. Just know it has nothing to do with you but their own limiting beliefs. Never let your own light dim to protect others from not feeling good. The only way you can help others is by following the path that has the most light for you.

Also know and remember that when we grow, we run into new obstacles. Sometimes, we think that when we get there everything will be solved and we can live peacefully until the end of our life. I used to think this. But because we live in this universe with both polarity and pure potentiality and are constantly expanding, your nonphysical being will keep asking for more. When you ask for more, you will be reminded of what you do not know or can't do yet. That feels like resistance and limitation until you remember to ask for help. Ask the universe and the right person will show up and teach you what you now are ready to learn. This is the onion. We keep peeling layers to get to know ourselves and become closer and close to the essence of who we really are. Pure love and potentiality.

So when we look out at the world and other people, remember that what you see is a reflection of you. This is the final universal law I will share with you as I promised to in Chapter 3: The Law of Reflection. Everyone around you are a reflection of you and your life. Lean into the wisdom of knowing that the obstacles you meet are there for you to peel another layer off. It is your chance to know what to ask for. When you do that with deliberate intention, feel how it feels to already have it. Allow it to come in whatever form it may be, appreciate the abundance you are surrounded with, and feel excited by all the pure potentiality ahead of you while you detach from when and where things will happen in life. Imperfectly perfect.

Chapter Twelve

Conclusion

Congratulations for making it to the end of the book! That tells me a lot about you and that you are serious about creating a life that you truly are proud of with the good and the bad showing up. All is well. You will be the best role model for your kids moving forward, because you now know how to fully step into your own power and make things happen the way you want.

Moving forward, you know that the universe has your back and how to work with this unlimited source of support and not against what you really want. Money does not have a meaning, and so it is now time to celebrate every coin rolling into your life and be excited about making more.

In order to make your life the way you want it, you will now focus on the clarity and pay attention how things will start to shift in your life.

To be a stronger magnet to all that you want to manifest in your life, you will let go of all the unwanted. Start upgrading your life and be the person you want to be before you actually get there. This will speed up the process. While you work toward your inner alignment and take the inspired action, know that it is about both relaxing and taking action. Do not fall into the trap of continuing to think your way through, but grab the phone and call the person you were thinking about who may be able to help you connect with the person in the company you want to work for. Or send that email out to the person who you know can help you set up your company and answer the questions that will make you feel at peace that you do it correctly.

While you now start to change your life, you know the importance of caring about your inner dream like a newly planted seed. You will find the best people you can think about to support you and know also to set boundaries. This is so important. By remembering this part, it will save you so much frustration of having to keep pulling yourself up because you will have those people in your support system that you know always will have your back.

When you now are on this journey, you are prepared for obstacles that will come up. It may not always be disasters. Life happens. If you stick to your success habits and keep building yourself up more and more resiliently, just remember that what shows up is a mirror of you. You can pivot this. Be patient. I know people who have been in the personal development field for decades and are still afraid. I feel it every day. It is like an onion. There will be layers we can keep peeling off until the day we finish this life journey.

As you move forward, I wish for you to have patience and to learn one thing at a time, just like children naturally do, before adults and society make them do it differently. We all will experience falling out of the connection with the powerful women we are.

I wish you will from now on believe in divine timing and that you are supported. Your only job is to ask and receive.

Acknowledgments

Since I was very little, I have been fascinated with books and from an early age I have thought about how cool it is when people take the time to put their stories and wisdom together into a book that other people can then enjoy. In my adult life, when I started to learn things I knew would benefit others, the desire to write a book began to brew inside of me. Several people have mentioned and suggested that I should become an author and write a book. I do believe that by connecting with other people throughout my life, I have gained experience, knowledge, and wisdom preparing me to give birth to this book. I will now take a few pages to acknowledge those I find have been catalysts and influential for the person I have become and the creation of this book.

The day I decided and felt in the bones of my body I would get this book written was this past fall of 2018. I had just given my dear friend Marion Toms a book as a thank you for a nice gesture. Her response to me was "You should write a book," while she looked me deep into the eyes. *Bam* – that was the moment I decided to do it now.

Of course I want to thank those who have trusted me as my clients and choose to be in my professional circle.

My intimate family, my husband Brian, and my kids: Nikolai, Rebekka, and Mathias. They were the first to hear of my decision. For the nine weeks it took for me to get my manuscript submitted they were pivotal in the support I received. My family is just perfectly imperfectly wonderful. I love our extension with Rebekka's Ty and Mathias's Kate. Also my first dog ever and furry soul buddy Maggie has to have her name mentioned.

My life all started because my mother decided to give birth to me though I came into her life when she was very young. She has shown me how strong we women really can be. I am forever grateful to her for daring to be different and choosing to keep me as her child.

My dad, who adopted me and chose to be the father I so desperately wanted. Today he is one of my heroes and with him I received an amazing extended family, especially Anne and Bjørn, who have been pivotal in how I experienced what is possible to have in a family life.

My brother, Lars, for allowing me to become close in our relationship as adults. I did not know how to be a loving sister when we were kids, but pretty much wanted to be the boss lady. I love you, brother, for the way you show up in life. I love your kids and Stephanie.

Mormor og morfar in heaven for spreading out your wings and giving me a safe loving home the first years of my life. I am grateful for the infinite connection we have.

Moster Lene for being there for me from I was a baby and still being my sister-aunty Lene. You have given me so much. I will always hold you close in my heart.

My uncle Carsten, who was like a brother to me and now in heaven and aunt Marianne. You always have cared so sincerely about my family and I. I value our connection and the guidance I receive from you whenever I reach out.

My uncle, Mogens, for sharing your wish for me before you chose to leave this life. I know you loved me and I remember how safe I felt when I could spend time with you.

My cousins and their families.

With my My family-in-law I enjoy how we all get together.

Vibeke Lind, Gitte Hansen, Marcie Spreen, and Erika Persson, you all have a very special trusted part of my heart.

Cathrine Prestroenning, Pia Steidel, Anette Sanchez, Diana Noble, Marion Toms, you are all proof that friends can show up and be part of life suddenly and genuinely.

Through non-profit work I have met countless amazing people who I have learned from and been inspired by. Some especially to mention are Ellen Malka, Tanya Andrews, Wendy Sheppard, and Rhonda Bible.

Birthe & Olai Kofoed, Pernille Blidsøe, Lene Nyborg, Marianne Pedersen, Hanne & Søren Storgaard, Signe and Daniel Hansen, Charlotte & Michael Reffstrup, Amanda Paris, and Rikke Falkenberg you have all impacted my life.

I could literally list 100+ other important friends and people who have impacted my life short term or long term here: Torben Hansen, Kirsten and Michael Poulsen, Inger & Jørgen Lind, Steven and Susan Perry, Lawrence and Kelly Boyle, Ward and Sharon Bennett, Gus & Robyn Suarez, Raj & Narida Hingoo, Sonali Ravindrakumar, Miko Liou, Rhonda Sternberg, Nanna Andersen, Hanne Marie Frostlid, Xiomar Eyzaguirre, Margie Mader, Katherine Baez, Amy Vignola, Åsa Bagley, Stacy Weisberg, Beth Rose, Caryn Cipes, Holly Erskine, Malinda Chamberland, Luz Manausa, Chris & Jennifer

Mackenzie, Craig Rumsky, Bindu Nair, Donna Levy, Tim Mullally, David & Barbara Maggiore, Shawn and Kerry Cerra, Gina Sinnott, Gloria Justiniano-Pareja, Grace Levy, Kelley Sorensen, Maria Schaff, Marie-Josee Berard, Roosevelt Jean-Francois, Shakira Taylor, Lydia Harris, Mary Landgraf, Family Kinsey, Matthew Parry, Grand Master Park, Master Yoe, Master E, Merete Mortensen, and Leah McCarthy.

My colleagues at ExpatRide have reminded me how important being on a team is for me.

From other interests and involvements in our community I have also been gifted by getting to know:

My miracle group, Gail, Jan and Jane

Health Professionals who especially have made a difference in my life are Bo Brooks, Sharon Miller, and Liz Olivas.

Of School employees I want to mention Nicole Beaney, Kelly Cummins, Lori Engasser, Mrs. Naik, Ms. Hoffmann, Mrs. Erich, and Mrs. Melamed

Throughout the years I have learned from many teachers:

My NLP Master Practitioner teachers, Pernille Bretton-Meyer and Rikke Loeb, who taught me to own my power and take responsibility for my past, present and future.

My NLP co-student Sofia Manning who I through our NLP studies am forever grateful for the conversations we had. She invited me to her first coaching program that she brought to Denmark after working for Antony Robbins. This planted the seed in me to know that coaching would always be a part of my professional life.

Christy Whitman came into my life when I decided that now was the time to start my career again and go deeper with my coaching skills. It didn't take long before I realized I had opened up to receive teachings and guidance that I never had imagined possible. From her teaching in the QSCA and the further coaching, mentoring, and training I have done with her, I have learned to not just connect with my own divine power but now I can also guide others in connecting with this true essence of who they are. The teacher who guided me through the first year in the QSCA is the one and only Julie Kleinhans who I have kept close to my heart.

From the QSCA, I have met so many amazing soul sisters and brothers. In particular I want to mention Beth Meyers, Jason Richardson, Roger Dawson, Jo Ellen Newman, Adriana Carballo, Isabel Stål, and Beverly Roberts.

Part of my journey to becoming more confident in public speaking in English has been by joining Toastmasters. Here I in particular want to thank Lois Margolin who has been my mentor.

I see myself as a lifelong learner and I always study inspirational leaders and teachers material, read books, and listen to podcasts or YouTube videos. Those who I often refer back to and who have impacted my life the most are: Christy Whitman whom was also mentioned earlier, Oprah Winfrey, Depak Chopra, Marie Forleo, Denise Duffield-Thomas, Ryan Eliason, Lewis Howes, John Lee Dumas, Lisa Sasevich, Steven Covey, David Bach, Brené Brown, Ester and Jerry Hicks, Sanaya Roman & Duane Packer, Marci Shimoff, Debra Poneman, Nick Ortner, Joe Vitale, Elisabeth Purvis, Christian Mickelsen, Tony Robbins, Brendon Burchard, and Jenifer Mclean.

I want to give a shout out to Angela Lauria and The entire Author Incubator Team. With your support I have had a safe place to give birth to this book in a shorter time than I thought possible. The support from Ora North in the pre-writing phase and Moriah Howell during the writing and editing phase has been tremendous.

For the creation of this printed book I want to acknowledge the Morgan James Publishing Team: David

Hancock, CEO & Founder; my Author Relations Manager, Tiffany Gibson; and special thanks to Jim Howard, Bethany Marshall, and Nickcole Watkins.

Thank you!

Thank You

Let's continue the conversation!

This isn't the end, but the beginning of a new journey of making your own money and mastering your life.

Reading a book is one way of learning new strategies and shifting the mindset of what is possible in life. The true change comes from integrating the steps and strategies you now have learned. For most people without support this can be the challenging part. If you would like to stay connected and make sure this will not just be another book where you learned a lot of profound and meaningful tools and habits, please go to my website www.charlottefriborg.com to learn more. You will also find out how you can continue the work.

I hope to see you there!

About the Author

Charlotte Friborg is the owner and CEO of Charlotte Friborg International LLC. When working with project leadership and integrating team building in England, as well as working in different employment bureaus in Denmark, Charlotte gained the interest in helping people bring out their best. After earning her NLP  Master Practitioner and her first coaching certification in Denmark, she started her own company. Her dream of staying home with her kids came true when she with her husband, Brian, and their three children moved to Florida. She earned her second coaching certification as a Law of Attraction life coach and also became a Light Body Meditation graduate in the US when she decided to start a career again.

During the years as a stay-at-home mom in the US, Charlotte volunteered for 1,000+ hours with various leadership roles. She also joined her kids in Taekwondo and earned a first-degree black belt with her kids. When the family expanded with their golden retriever, Maggie, Charlotte had Maggie pass the top test to become a Certified Therapy Dog, who she has worked with at an elementary school, a nursing home, and at Stoneman Douglas High School. Having studied and implemented various tools in her life for more than two decades helps her to live a life with 360-degree life mastery – perfectly imperfectly. The core of her work lies in integrating success habits with the universal principles that no one taught us about in school. She is a master at finding people's strengths and potential.

CPSIA information can be obtained
at www.ICGtesting.com
Printed in the USA
JSHW011237071222
34492JS00002B/355

9 781642 797336